YORKSHIRE

DIALECT

A Selection of Yorkshire
Words and Anecdotes

by
Louise Maskill

BRADWELL
BOOKS

Published by Bradwell Books
11 Orgreave Close Sheffield S13 9NP
Email: books@bradwellbooks.co.uk

British Library Cataloguing in Publication Data:
a catalogue record for this book is available from the
British Library.

1st Edition

ISBN: 9781902674650

Print: Gomer Press, Llandysul, Ceredigion SA44 4JL

Typesetting by: Andrew Caffrey

Photograph credits: Roger Maskill,
Sheffield Local Studies Library Picture Sheffield
& the Unnetie Digitisation Project.

YORKSHIRE DIALECT

by Louise Maskill

ACKNOWLEDGEMENTS

This book came together at the request and with the support of Chris Gilbert; I am indebted to him for research materials, guidance and for his faith in me. Tom, Molly, Owen and Caitlin have encouraged and supported me throughout and made their own contributions to the A-to-Z, as have various folk of Yorkshire extraction whom I've badgered for words. My thanks especially to Paul and Chandler.

My parents, proud Yorkshire folk, have provided anecdotes, memories, images and a good deal of moral support. My crack squad of readers – Roger, Bernice, Tom – found errors aplenty in early drafts; any that remain in the book are my responsibility, not theirs.

HUGE THANKS TO ALL OF YOU

DEDICATION

*For Gladys and Bernard,
Rita and Walter & Bernice and Roger;
my Yorkshire heritage*

> *Being from Yorkshire is as much a state of mind as a geographical fact.*
>
> LIAM ALLEN

Introduction

Although dialects are still evident in everyday speech from different parts of the country, they are nowhere near as common or as diverse as they used to be. This gradual extinction has been noted and mourned by writers and antiquarians over many years, and huge efforts have been made to capture the colloquial speech of men and women from all over Britain.

My grandparents and parents are proud Yorkshire folk from the West Riding, so even though I grew up as an immigrant in Norfolk I was surrounded by the Yorkshire accent and dialect at home and whenever we travelled up north to see my extended family. The research process for this book has triggered a great number of fond memories, and I can still hear the voices of my grandparents uttering many of the words and phrases to be found here.

The first part of this book is an A to Z of words and phrases arranged with their meanings and a few examples of usage, while the second part contains a collection of anecdotes, stories, rhymes and curiosities, all arranged by theme. Some of the words in the A to Z are now in common use in everyday English, but the aim is to indicate their provenance in the old Yorkshire dialect.

The anecdotes may be long or short, complicated or simple, but all contain genuine examples of Yorkshire dialect as gathered by myself or recorded by historians and collectors over the years.

I have revisited a lot of happy family memories in researching and collating this book. Along the way I have smiled, laughed, winced and (in one or two cases) blushed at the terminology used by down-to-earth Yorkshire men and women from years gone by. I hope this book might contribute in some small way to preserving a few of the words which were once in common use but which now face extinction.

A

Aback – behind, at the back of

Aboon – an excess of something

Ackers – money

Acting the goat – messing around, being stupid

Addle – earn

Afore – before

Agee – askew or crooked

Ah – I

Ailment – the standard term for a disease or illness
  What ails thee?

Alicker – vinegar

Alley-taw – a marble used in a children's game

Allus, awlus – always

An' all – as well

Anyroad – anyway, anyhow

Apiece – each

Arran – spider or spider's web

Arrered – beaten or defeated

Article – a person (mildly derogatory)

Arvill – a funeral

As snug as a bug in a rug – warm and cosy, especially while in bed or in wrapped up in warm clothing

Asker – a newt

Askings, askins – the marriage banns

Attercop – a spider

Aught – anything

Aum – an elm tree

Awd – old

Aye – yes

Ax – to ask

B

Ba'an, barn – a small child

Babberpants – cowardly

Backslaver – impudent, cheeky response

Badger – a dealer, pedlar or tradesman

Badly – feeling poorly, not so well. May be used in response to a greeting

Bahn – going

Ah'm noan bahn yonder – I'm not going over there

Baht – without

Bam – a trick or practical joke

Bank – a hill

Banter – to tread noisily or heavily

Bar – without

Barf – a long low hill

Barley – a term for a truce in a children's game

Barmpot – a silly fellow

Bassock – batter, thrash soundly

Bastile – the workhouse

Beck – a stream

Beet – to repair, especially of nets

Belike – probably

Bellikin – a puppy

Bellman – Yorkshire name for the ancient office of town crier, still maintained in Ripley

Belter – an exceptional example of something

Bensel or **bensil** – to beat or thrash

Besom – a twig broom, or a woman of flexible morals

Bezzle – to eat or drink greedily, or to squander

Biddy – a louse

Bide – to bear or put up with

Bield – shelter, living accommodation

> *When I were courtin' Mary Ann,*
> *T'owd squire, he says one day,*
> *"I've got no bield fer wedded fowks;*
> *Choose, wilt ta wed or stay?"*

>> *From A Dalesman's Litany:*
>> *From Hell, Hull and Halifax, good Lord deliver us*

Billy-biter – a bluetit

Blackbright – extremely dirty

Blackclock – the black beetle

Blain, blen – a stye or a sore around the eye

Blashy – wet, squally weather

Blazer – a sheet of metal held up against a fire grate to funnel a draught and cause the fire to flare up

Blether-skite – a gossip, a tattle-tale

Blish – a blister

Blood-alley – a red-streaked marble

Blowed – dumbfounded, astonished

Bluther – to weep noisily and ostentatiously

Bocken, boke – to retch or vomit

Body – a person

Life's troubles are oft ov a body's own makin'.

Bonny – (of a child or young woman) attractive, healthy-looking

Bottery – the elder tree

Bowdykite – a mischievous or unruly girl

Braid – to make or mend nets or crab pots

Bramble-nosed – possessed of a red or purple nose through the imbibing of too much alcoholic refreshment

Brass – money, coins

Bratted – (of milk or cream) just turning sour

Braying – hitting, beating, assaulting with fists

Breeks or **britches** – trousers

Brig – a promontory of land projecting into the sea

Brock – a badger

Broddle – to pick at or make holes in

Brokken – broken

Brussen – a useful word, meaning boastful, in possession of a lot of something, or full after over-eating

Buck – cheek or impudence

Bugger – a mild expletive commonly used by adults and children, with no sexual connotations. May also mean a rogue or likeable scamp

Bullspink – a bullfinch

Bullstang – a dragonfly

Bummelkite – a bumblebee, or sometimes a bramble bush

Buzzard – a nocturnal moth

By gum! – by God! My word, fancy that!

By heck! – by Hell! A stronger exclamation than by gum

Byre – cow-shed

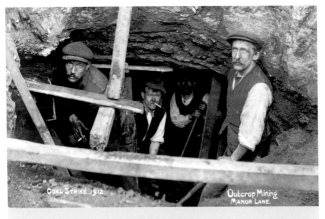

Outcrop mining at Manor Lane, Sheffield during a coal strike in 1912

C

Cack – excrement

Cadely – in delicate or precarious health

Caff – to give up or give in. Hence caff hearted – cowardly

Cake-oile – the mouth

Call – to criticise

Canned – drunk, intoxicated

Canny – careful, shrewd

Canty – brisk, lively, cheerful

Cap – to top something off. Sometimes used as an exclamation of surprise

Ah wor fair capped!

Carlins – dried peas

Carr – marshy woodland

Case clock – a grandfather or grandmother clock

Catie-cornered – aslant, askew

Champion – very good, excellent

Chelp – to answer back or complain, especially used of children

Chevin – a ridge or edge of land. Often reflected in place names such as Otley Chevin

Chink – money, coins

Chippy – the starling

Chuffed – very pleased, delighted

Chuffed off – cross, disappointed

Chuffy – arrogant, haughty

Chunter – mutter, grumble

Clack – gossip

Clap cold – stone cold, used especially of food

Clarty – smeared with dirt or grease

Clashy – stormy weather

Cleg – a horsefly

Clew – a ball of yarn

Clog – a traditional wooden-soled shoe.
The basis of many expressions:

> *pop yer clogs* (die)
>
> *as dry as a lime-burner's clog* (extremely thirsty)
>
> *clog on* (keep going)

Clouts – underwear

Cobby – active, energetic

Coil – coal

Coilskep – coal scuttle

Collier – a coal miner

Common as muck – derogatory phrase used to describe a vulgar person

Conny – dear, darling

Cop – to catch

> *Tha'll cop it* (you'll be in trouble)
>
> *Cop 'old an' stick* (grab hold and don't let go)

Cot – knot or tangled hank of hair.
Hence *cottered, cottery* – tangled, matted

Courtin' – close relationship prior to engagement and marriage

Tha's been a'courtin' Mary Jane!

    (First verse of On Ilkley Moor Baht 'At)

Cow-clap – a cow pat

Creel – a bench for killing pigs

Creep-hole – a hole made in a drystone wall to allow sheep to pass through

Cronk – to huddle or crouch, especially for warmth

Cuddy – a donkey, or sometimes a hedge sparrow

Cussen – dark, gloomy and overcast

Cut – a canal

Cutter – soft, gentle, lilting talk

D

Dacky – a pig

Dad – a lump of slice of something, e.g. bread

Daffly – confused or senile

Daized – numb with cold

Darkening – twilight

Darking – eavesdropping

Dashery – housework

Deck – to give up or give in, especially in the face of too much food or too much work or effort

Delf – a quarry

Delver – a quarryman

Demmock – a diseased or bruised spot on a potato

Dicky – a louse; or rickety, shaky

Ding – to strike or hit

Dobber – a large marble

Doddy – a cow or bull without horns

Doit – a finger, or a state of forgetfulness caused by old age

Donnakin – earth closet or privy

Doorstone – a doorstep

Dorp – a carrion crow

Dossn't, dursn't – dare not

Dowled – flat, especially of liquor

Dowly – low-spirited

Drop o' York – the hangman's scaffold on the Knavesmire in York

Droy – dry, thirsty

Druffen – drunk, intoxicated

Dub – puddle or pool

Duff-up – a fight or brawl

Duffy – doughy and underbaked

Durdam – commotion, chaos

Dwamy, dwalmy – faint, lightheaded

Cottage garden outside a house in Grimesthorpe, around 1900

E

Ee! – a useful all-purpose utterance, employed for emphasis, to signify disbelief, relief, happiness and any number of other emotions and responses

Een or ees – eyes

Efter – after

Eld, elder – as eld means as soon as, would prefer to
Ah'd as eld do wi'out as pay yon price.

Eldin, eldrin, edlring – kindling, firewood

Eller – the elder tree

16

Emmot – ant
'En-'oile – a chicken run
Enow – enough, sufficient
Esh – the ash tree
Ey up! – a useful exclamation which can be used in surprise, to warn someone to look out, or as a greeting

F

Faffin' – messing about with
Fain – glad, very pleased
Fair – really, completely
Fause – shrewd, cunning
Fantickles – facial freckles
Fell – hill, especially in rough moorland
Fent – odd remnant of cloth
Ferrie or foggie – the one who goes first in a children's game
Fetch – bring, carry along
Fettle – originally a textile term meaning to comb, but now may mean to clean and tidy *(fettle up)*, to finish a job, or to sort someone out *(Ah'll fettle thee!)*
Fettlin' day – cleaning day, usually Friday
Firepoint – a poker
Fit – ready, prepared
Flacker – to tremble or flutter

Flaycrow – scarecrow

Flaysome – terrifying, dreadful

Fleck-lenny – a chaffinch

Fleet, flet – a fire, or glowing embers

Flig – to fly. Hence *fligged*, *fledged* or *feathered*.

Flish – a blister

Flither – a limpet

Flittermouse – a bat

Flower – a fond term of address

Nah then, my flower!

Flummoxed – bamboozled, at a loss

Foggie – to go first in a children's game

Foisty – musty, turning bad

Foomart – a stoat or polecat

Forkin'-robin – an earwig

Frame thissen! – get yourself organised!

Fresh – new

Owt fresh? – any news?

Fret – worry

Frit – scared or frightened

Frosk – a frog

Fuddle – a party or entertainment, usually with food
and drink

Funny-ossity – an eccentric person; someone with odd or
curious behaviour

Fetching water from Wild Well, Norton Hollow

G

Gab – to chatter idly

Gammerstang – a woman or girl of dubious morals

Gammy – lame or injured

Gansey – a traditional fisherman's pullover

Gate – road or way

Gaum – common sense. Hence *gaumless* (sometimes spelled *gormless*) – foolish or lacking in common sense

Gauve – to stare

Get shut on – get rid of a possession

Getten – got

Gill (pronounced 'jill') – a half-pint

Gimmer – a female lamb

Ginnel – an alleyway between two houses.
Usually narrow, sometimes covered over
He couldn't stop a pig in a ginnel – that man is rather
bow-legged

Gippy – a starling

Gi'ower! – stop that!

Gizzen – to cry, grizzle

Glave – (of weather) cold and shivery

Glee – to squint

Goit – channel of water

Goodies – sweeties

Goosegogs – gooseberries

Goster – to bluster or talk loudly

Gowk – the cuckoo

Gowldy – the yellowhammer

Gradeley – fine, excellent, very good

Graithe – riches, wealth

Grand – very good, excellent

Grid – a bicycle

Growler – a pork pie

Grum – angry or grim

Grundid – buried underground

Gumption – common sense

Guytresh – an imp or evil spirit

H

Hackle – clothing. Hence hackled – dressed up

Hagg – a division of a piece of woodland; the part which is about to be felled

Hagworm – snake or adder

Haig – a haw, the fruit of the hawthorn

Hallack – to dawdle or lag behind

Halsh – a noose or knot in a rope

Happen – maybe, perhaps

Happen on – to come across or discover

Harr – a misty, foggy drizzle

Hasta? – Have you?

Hask – rough or coarse

Haugh – a steep hill

Heart-sluffened – heartbroken, very miserable

Hell's bells and buckets o' blood – exclamation of surprise and annoyance

Helm – a shed

Helte – knot, tangle, confusion

Hesp – a catch or latch

Hig – temper, irritation; or a short sharp rainshower

Hissen, hersen – himself, herself

Hob – a sprite or goblin

Hollin – holly

Hook – a conman or shady type

How – a hill

Huggin – an armful

Huggermugger – a muddle or a tangle

Hutch up – request to move up a little on a seat or bench

Orgreave Colliery during the 1893 coal strike

I

Idle – lazy, indolent

Idle-back – a lazy person, or a fisherman's term for a rod-rest

Ill-thriven – malnourished, underfed

Ing – a water meadow

Intake – land reclaimed for farming from rough moorland

Ivin – ivy

Ivver – ever

J

Jag – a load

Jannock – fair, right, correct

Jart – to hit

Jay-legged – knock-kneed

Jenny-spinner – a cranefly or daddy-longlegs

Jeremy Joy – the common thrush

Jerry – a chamberpot

Jiggered – tired out, exhausted

Jip – severe pain

Jonkin – a tea party to celebrate the birth of a baby

Joskin – a country worker

Joss – to bounce up and down

Jotherum – a quivering, wobbly mass

Jubberty – an obstacle or annoyance

Judycow – the ladybird

Jumble – a traditional gingerbread cake dusted in sugar

Just now – at once, directly; or in a moment

K

Kale – porridge or broth

Kall – to chat or gossip

Kecks – trousers or underpants

Kedd – a sheep louse

Keld, kell – a spring or well

Kelter – rubbish, refuse

Kenspeck – a distinguishing mark. Hence *kenspeckled*, having a noticeable peculiarity

Keslop – rennet, used in making cheese

Kest – a slight squint

Ket – carrion, offal

Ketty – rancid or nasty

Kibble – to grind into small pieces

Kick out can – a children's game

Kincough – a whooping cough

Kist – wooden chest or trunk

Kittle – to tickle

Kizzened – withered, wizened

Knackered – very tired

Knackin' – affected way of speaking

Knapper – a door knocker

Knobble – to hit with a stick

Knur and spell – an adults' game

Kye – cattle, cows

Kysty – hard to please, quick to find fault

The Old Cross Scythes pub, Woodseats

L

Lace – to thrash or beat

Lad – boy, young man

Lady-cow – the ladybird

Lagged – tired out

Laggie – the last to take a turn in a children's game

Laithe – barn

Lake or laik – to be out of work, or to play.
Hence *laikin'* – playing
Lame under t'cap – a little slow on the uptake
Lamping – poaching
Land – to hit, catch with a blow; or to arrive somewhere
Lant – urine
Lanty – someone who is habitually late
Lass – girl, woman. Often used for young children,
but may be applied to women of any age as a term of
endearment
Latt – a thin strip of wood, such as might be used in a
ceiling or fence panel
Ee, she were as thin as a latt.
Laverock – the skylark
Leap – a large deep wicker basket
Learn – to teach, as well as the more traditional meaning
Ah learned 'im all 'e knowed
Leg it – to walk or run fast
Legger – a man who propels a barge through a narrow canal
tunnel by lying on his back and 'walking' along the walls
Lennock – supple or pliant
Let on – to tell, reveal (especially a secret – *Don't thee
let on!*)
Lig, ligg – lie, recline
Ling – heather, or a type of slender sea-fish
Lip – insolent backchat, verbal cheek

Lolling – slouching, lying

Lolly – the tongue

Lop – a flea; hence loppy, dirty and fleariddden. Also a fisherman's term for an ocean chop or swell

Love, luv – affectionate term of address, used for both males and females

Lownd – (of the sea) calm and peaceful

Lug – ear

Lum – a chimney

Lunt – light or flame

Lye – scythe

M

Maddle – to confuse or puzzle. Hence *maddlin*, a fool or one who is easily confused

Maiden – a wooden clothes horse

Main – very

Mak, mek – to make

Manky – scruffy, dirty, rotten

Mar – lake or mere

Mardy – sulky, grumpy; or, of a child, spoilt or indulged

Marlock, mullock – to play pranks or mess around

Marrish – marsh, or land liable to flooding

Mash – to brew or brew tea

Maul abaht – to manhandle or handle roughly

Maunsell – a dirty, slovenly, lazy person (especially a woman)

Mawkin – a scarecrow

Mawkish – descriptive of a person who is always whining or complaining

Mazzen – to daydream

Meg – a ha'penny.

I 'aven't a meg to me name.

Mell – to meddle or interfere

Mend – to replace or replenish; or to improve in health after an illness

Ee, mend the fire, it's nitherin' in 'ere.

Mense – decency, tidiness, neatness. Hence menseless, untidy, indecent

Mention – a small amount, especially of food

Aye, go on then, ah'll just tek a mention

Mickle – much, more than

Middlin' – about average, neither good nor bad

Mind! – take notice of what I'm telling you!

Mint – to faint

Mipe – to sneak or move silently and furtively

Missen, missel – myself

Mistal – cow-shed

Mizzle – very fine drizzle combined with a mist or fog

Moither – to fluster, pester or muddle

Mop – a coastal term for a small codfish

Mort – an abundance, a great amount

Moss – bog or marsh
Mowdiwarp – a mole
Muck – dirt, rubbish, grime
Muddly – close and humid
Mullock – a mess, a blunder
Mun – must
Munt – mustn't

York Minster and city walls

N

Nabbins – term of endearment, especially for a child

Nack – a round shallow depression scooped out of the ground for the game of taws

Nanpie – a magpie

Nantle – to move slowly and aimlessly; to potter

Napper – the head

Natter – to have a long chat, or to irritate or annoy

Nay – no

Near – tight-fisted, parsimonious with money

Neave or neeaf – fist

Near – parsimonious or sparing with money

Neb – the peak of a cap, or a nose or beak

Nelly – umbrella

Nerks – chips

Nesh – soft, weak, apt to feel the cold. May be applied to children or southern folk

Netty or nessy – a toilet, particularly an outside privy

Nicely – feeling well, healthy. May be used in response to a greeting

Nip-curn, nip-screw or nip-scrote – a miser or mean person

Nitherin' – bitterly cold

Nobbut – only-

Ay, I know we're nobbut farmers,
Mowin' gerse an' tentin' kye,
But we're proud of all we've stood fer
I'yon ages that's gone by.
   From Cambodunum

Nointer – to potter about

Nor – than

Norpins – money, especially small change

Nowt – nothing

Nuppit – simpleton or fool; or a mischievous child

O

Offald – tired and dirty

Off-comed-uns – foreigners, folk from outside Yorkshire or newcomers to the district

Oile – hole. Various usages – *coil-oile* (coal hole), *lug-oile* (earhole), and curiously *chip-oile* (fish-and-chip shop)

Ommust – almost, nearly

On – of

Once ovver – formerly, once upon a time

Orts – leftovers from a meal

Ossin' ter slaht – coming on to rain

Over-faced – presented with too much to eat

Over many – too many, an unnecessary abundance

Our – a term used to indicate relationship within a family.
May be applied to offspring, cousins, siblings –
our Mary, our Howard
Outgang – the exit or way out
Owd Nick, Owd Scrat, t'Owd Lad – the Devil
Ower – over, too
Own – to recognise or acknowledge
Owt – anything
Owt like – reasonable, fit, in good health
Oxter – the armpit

Haymaking at Creswick's Farm, Crosspool

P

Paddle – to slip or slide, especially in mud

Pafty – cheeky, impudent

Paigle – the cowslip

Pairt – quite a lot of

Palaver – fuss, unnecessary time-wasting

Palm – pussy-willow with catkins, used for decoration on Palm Sunday

Pap – teat

Parkin – a cake made from oats, ginger and treacle. Traditionally eaten on Plot or Mischief Night (November 5th)

Parky – chilly, cold

Parzle – to wander or stroll slowly and cautiously

Pash – a shower of rain

Patty – a Yorkshire speciality, a battered fishcake made from fish sandwiched between slices of potato

Pawky – shrewd, cunning

Peff – a slight, tickly and persistent cough, or to breathe in short gasps

Pen – a hill. Often reflected in place names

Penk – to inspect sneakily

Piece – a length of cloth

Pynot – a magpie

Pike – a stye or pustule

Pikelet – the Yorkshire name for a crumpet

Pine, pined – to be hungry or in need of sustenance

Plague – to tease

Pleeaf – plough

Plisky – trick, jape or escapade

Plothery or pluthery – muddy

Plotter – to walk or wade through mud

Pobs, pobbies – soft food given to children or invalids, e.g. bread soaked in warm sweetened milk

Popped up – drunk, replete with ale

Porriwiggle – a tadpole

Potless – without money

Pots – the washing up

Powk – a stye or sore on the eye

Puddled – dim or slow-witted

Q

Quarrel – a flagstone, or sometimes a glass pane

Queer stick – an odd or eccentric person

Quicks – hawthorn saplings used for hedge-laying

Quicksticks – to do something fast or instantly

R

Raddle – to beat or thrash

Raggald – a ruffian or thug

Ranty – wild, boisterous, excited

Rasselled – withered, shrivelled

Rat-arsed – falling-over drunk

Ratcher – a tall story or fabrication

Rawk – mist or drizzle. Hence rawky, damp and misty

Reckon – to evaluate or weigh up, or to pretend

Renky – tall and athletic

Renny – a fox

Renny-tails – foxgloves

Rick – smoke

Rifting – belching or passing wind

Rigweltered – (of animals) on their backs with their feet in the air, unable to get up

Rive – to tear

Rizzom – a tiny scrap

Road – way or method

You're goin' abaht it wrong road.

Roaring – weeping, crying

Roke – a dense rolling sea fog that often reaches far inland

Roister – a noisy wailing child

Ronce – to climb up something

Rops – the guts or entrails of a butchered animal

Rosined – rosy with ale

Ruddock – the robin

Rue – to regret something

Ruttle – the rattling noise made by an asthmatic or cold-sufferer when they breathe

An open-air service in the East End of Sheffield, 1920s

S

Sad – poorly risen, as with cakes or bread

Saim – cooking fat or lard

Sam – to gather up or collect things together

Sark – a shirt

Saur – cess, slurry, liquid manure

Scarborough woof – a variety of catfish, especially common in the waters off Scarborough

Scarpy – (of soil) dry and stony

Scoddy – poor or meagre

Scollops – thick slices of potato, battered and deep-fried

Scran – food

Scraps – the bits of batter left behind in a chip fryer. A chip-oile delicacy

Cod 'n' chips twice 'n' a bag o' scraps, please.

Scroggin' – gathering, as of berries etc.

Scutter – excrement

Seg – a metal stud for reinforcing the soles of shoes to minimise wear; or an animal that has been gelded

Seggie – the second child to take a turn in a game

Set – to lay the table, or to sow seeds

Shackle – the wrist

Shambles – a name given to some Yorkshire streets (in York, Wetherby and Kirbymoorside); originally meant street-side meat stalls

Sharn – cow dung

Sheddler – a swindler or con man

Shent ower – overcast, cloudy

Sheppy, shepster – a starling

Shift thissen! – come on, get a move on!

Shive – a thick slice (or meat or bread)

Shiver – a very thin slice

Shog – to walk slowly or uncertainly

Shold – slipper

Shot – to get shot of something means to get rid of it

Siling – pouring down with rain

Simmeron – a wild primrose

Sind – to rinse or wash out

Sipe – to ooze or drain slowly

Sithee! – listen here! Used to draw attention and emphasise a point

Skell – to tip or spill

Skeller – to squint, or to warp or twist (especially of wood)

Skelp – to beat or thrash; a skelping was a corporal punishment

Skep – a basket

Skew-whiff – aslant, crooked

Skimmer – to glint or shimmer

Skitters – diarrhoea

Slack – hollow or depression in the ground; or coal dust and tiny bits of coal

Slipe – to shave off

Slive – to move stealthily

Slops – trousers

Sluffed – upset or annoyed

Slug – to destroy

Snap – a West Riding term for a miner's lunch, often carried in a tin box

Snattle – to fritter away

Sneck – a door latch

Snicket – a narrow alleyway

Snickle – a snare, like that used by a poacher

Snided – infested, as with fleas or greenfly

Snizy – bitingly cold

Soft – weak, cowardly, foolish

Spell – a splinter of wood in the flesh

Spice – sweeties, confectionery

Spink – a chaffinch

Sprog – to spit; or a young child or baby

Starved – perishing with cold

Stee – ladder

Steg – a gander

Sticks – to make sticks was to split logs for kindling

Stopping – staying, remaining

   Sit dahn and tek thi coat off, look as if tha's stoppin'.

Strickle – sharpening tool or whetstone

Suited – pleased, happy about something

Summat – something
Sweel – to gutter or flicker, as a candle
Syke – a small stream, gutter or channel for water

A woman walking in the Rivelin Valley

T

Tack – food of inferior quality

Taffled – tangled or knotted

Taistrel – a scoundrel, rascal

Tanner – a sixpence

Taws – marbles

Where's our Roger?

'E's laikin' taws in t'ginnel.

Teem – to pour out (from a teapot); or to rain heavily

Tek off – to imitate the actions or idiosyncrasies
of another

Telltale tit – a sneak, a disloyal person

Telltale tit, yer tongue'll split…

Teng – to sting

Testril – a badly-behaved child

Tewit – a lapwing

Tewtle – to snow very lightly

That – very; used for emphasis

He were that mean; It is that.

Thee, tha, thine – you, your, yours

Them – those

Think on! – an admonishment, firmly recommending
that the offender should consider the error of their ways

Thissen – yourself

Thoil – endure, bear

I can't thoil t'brass – I can't bring myself to spend my money on that rubbish

Thrang or throng – busy

She were as throng as Throp's wife.

Throssie, throstle – the song thrush

Timpy-toed – walking with the feet turned inward; pigeon-toed

Tod – a fox

Tom Pudding – a coal barge plying Yorkshire's canals to serve the power stations

Tommy – nonsense, rubbish

Toom – empty

Tow – mess or muddle; or to play the fool

Stop towin' abaht.

Traps – belongings, worldly goods

Trod – a footpath

Turn – an entertainer. Family parties or gatherings sometimes involved everyone standing up to 'do a turn'

Tusky – rhubarb

Tussy peg or toothy peg – a tooth

Twinge, twitchbell – an earwig

Twitchel – a narrow pasageway

Tyke – dog, or a small child. Sometimes extended to become an affectionate name for all Yorkshiremen

U

Uking – an itch

Ullett, ullott – a baby owl

Unbethink – to change one's mind

Unkerd – strange, ghostly, eerie

Unkers – thighs or haunches

Unsneck – to unlatch a door

Up sticks – come on, let's get on our way

Upgang – an uphill road or trackway

Urchin – hedgehog

Us – our

We're goin' on us 'olidays.

Ussen – ourselves

Uzzle – a blackbird

V

Vast 'o – very many, a huge amount

Vennel – sink or drain

Viewsome, viewly – attractive or good-looking

The pit head at Tinsley Park Colliery

W

Waif 'n' straif – flotsam and jetsam washed up on the beach

Wallop – thrash, inflict physical punishment

Wame – stomach or belly

Wang – to throw hard and with determination

Warf – tasteless or bland; musty

Warve – to turn left

Wathstead – a ford

Watter wallops – boiled dumplings

Weatherglass – a barometer

Wed – married

Welt – to hit or thrash

Wesp – a wasp

Wessies – people from the West Riding

Wham – swampy, marshy land

While – until

Whinny – gorse or furze

Whisht – be quiet, silence

White over – a light covering of snow

Whittle – a knife

Wick – smart, energetic, streetwise; or crawling with something, e.g. vermin

Widdy – the willow tree

Witheren or wrezzle – a weasel

Wittering – nattering, annoying idle chit-chat

Wolsh – flavourless

Wreet – a wheelwright

Wuthering – (of the wind) tempestuous; descriptive of the sound the wind makes as it howls through trees and round buildings

X, Y, Z

Yacker – an acre

Yackron – an acorn

Yaffle – the green woodpecker

Yak – the oak tree

Yal – ale, beer

Yam – home

Yanly, yannerly – alone, solitary

Yark – to tug or pull fiercely

Yat – gate

Yersel, yersen – yourself

Yesterneet – last night

Yewer – a cow's udder

Yitten – scared, cowardly

Yon – that person or thing over there

Yonderly – preoccupied, having a faraway look in one's eyes

Youth – any slightly disreputable fellow, applied irrespective of age

Pronunciation and usage

The first thing any *off-comed-un* (a foreigner from outside Yorkshire or a newcomer to an area) needs to learn is how to pronounce the name of their newly adopted county. As any Yorkshire native knows, it's not Yorkshyre (to rhyme with hire) or Yorksheere (to rhyme with near), but *Yorksher*, to rhyme with huh. Any other variation will immediately indicate foreign origins or (possibly) pretensions to grandeur. A similar rule applies to the pronunciation of Harrogate – anything other than *'Arragut* will be frowned upon.

Yorkshire is the largest county in the UK; with an area of just over six thousand square miles it is almost twice the size of the next largest counties (Ross and Argyll in Scotland, both encompassing just over three thousand square miles). Yorkshire is so large that historically it has been divided into three smaller administrative areas, the West, East and North Ridings, as well as the Ainsty of York. The word *riding* is Viking in origin, harking back to the county's Norse heritage and deriving from the word *threthingr,* meaning a third part.

Farming in Robin Hood's Bay

In terms of dialect, the county may be divided roughly into two, with West Riding dialect being distinct in a number of ways from the dialect spoken in the East and North Ridings. There are some pronunciation differences – for example, a West Riding native might say *dahn* for down, while an East or North Riding resident would say *doon*. Similarly, a West Riding speaker's coat would be named a *coit*, while an East or North Riding person would call for their *cooat*. The West Riding is acknowledged to have a hard, almost brash sound, while the North and East Ridings have a softer dialect, perhaps because of its more rural origins. The differences may also stem back to linguistic distinctions between the ancient British kingdoms of Mercia (to which much of the West Riding once belonged) and Northumbria (which encompassed the majority of the East and North Ridings).

The Yorkshire dialect and accent are often utilised on film and in television, portraying a certain grittiness of character, friendliness, stoicism and a no-nonsense approach to life, combined with down-to-earth humour and a strong dash of bloody-minded stubbornness. The use of *thee*, *tha* and *thine* instead of you, your and yours is generally taken to be a defining characteristic of the Yorkshire dialect, but it is a fact little known outside Yorkshire that the use of these terms is in fact reserved for relations and friends, and over-use with folk outside these close social relationships is seen as inappropriately familiar. In the West Riding an overly-familiar person might be told:

Ee, dooan't thee thee-tha me! Tha thee-tha's them as thee-tha's thee!

The other defining characteristic is the glottal stop, written as t', which often stands in for *the* or *to*. It is sometimes difficult for non-Yorkshire folk to imitate, especially in phrases with lots of hard sounds such as *shut t'door* or *trouble at t'mill*. Yorkshire speech also has a number of characteristic phrases, some of which have entered the national lexicon and many of which would be understandable to most people these days. *Ey up!* is an example of a phrase which has come to signify the Yorkshireman in the media and in popular culture, as is *Nah then*. However, a foreigner's ear might well lose the subtleties of expression or emphasis which can give this phrase in particular a variety of different meanings. *Nah, then?* is a friendly greeting, while *Nah **then!*** means here we are, but ***Nah then!*** means watch out, that's enough!

Yorkshire has a wide variety of terrains, from the flat arable lands towards the east coast, through the rolling Dales and up onto the wild northern moors. Before the Industrial Revolution the county's farming heritage gave rise to a rich vocabulary of terms for weather. Rain might be *mizzly, silin' it dahn*, or *comin dahn like stair rods*. If it was bitterly cold it might be *nitherin'*, and if there was a light covering of snow one might say it was *white ower*. The approach of stormy or clashy weather might be noted over nearby hills with the phrase *it's black ower Bill's wife's mother's*.

Fishing in the River Swale at Low Row, a village in Swaledale

History, traditions and customs

The unofficial anthem of Yorkshire folk everywhere is *On Ilkla Moor Baht 'At*, a comedy song supposedly made up by the members of a church choir (probably from Halifax) during an outing to the famous Cow and Calf rocks on Ilkley Moor. It is sung to the tune of Cranbrook, a well-known hymn composed in 1805, and comprises a series of leg-pulling verses about a member of the choir who has been spotted returning from a tryst with Mary Jane, minus his hat.

The dialect verses run as follows:

Wheere wor ta bahn when Ah saw thee?
Oh Ilkla Moor baht 'at...
Tha's been a-courtin' Mary Jane
Tha's bahn ter get thi death o' cowd
Then we s'll 'a' ter bury thee
Then t'worms'll come ter eyt thee up
Then t'ducks'll come ter eyt up t'worms
Then we s'll come ter eyt up t'ducks
Then we s'll all 'ave etten thee
Then we s'll 'ave us ooan back!

The song has the advantage of going on for quite some time, with plenty of shouting and boisterous energy released during the chorus. How my parents must have enjoyed those long car journeys when my sisters and I would belt out *On Ilkla Moor Baht 'At* over and over again!

The Cow and Calf Rocks, Ilkley Moor

The social stereotype of a Yorkshireman with his whippet and flat cap stems back to the county's proud industrial and agricultural heritage. Another commonly attributed stereotype is the Yorkshireman's parsimony – he has been described as a Scotsman with the generosity squeezed out – and although this may be a little unfair, a careful examination of the Yorkshireman's motto does reveal an eye for keeping a close eye on one's brass (money):

'Ear all, see all, say nowt;

Eat all, sup all, pay nowt,

And if ever tha does owt for nowt,

Allus do it for thissen.

(Translation: hear everything, see everything, keep quiet; eat and drink well but pay nothing; and if you ever do something for nothing, make sure you do it for yourself.)

Lodge Moor

One elderly Yorkshireman was reported to always drink his pints *at yah sloup* (in one go). When he was asked why he always knocked back his drinks so quickly, his typically cautious reply was: *Aw, Ah yance 'ad yan knocked ower!*

In other, clearly inferior (and most likely jealous) parts of the country, a Yorkshireman is the name given to a fly drowned in a pint of beer, said to be a reference to the sharp and cadging nature of Yorkshire folk. However, as one Yorkshireman noted:

> *A chap can be too sharp sometimes. My advice is, be as sharp as ye like, if yer sharp in a reight way, but ther's some things it's as weel to be slow abaht. Be slow to do a shabby trick, an' be sharp to help a poor body 'at needs it. Be slow to see other fowk's faults, an' be sharp to improve yor own. Be slow to scandalise yor neighbours, an' keep a sharp luk aht to steer clear ov iverybody else's business; ye'll find it'll give ye mooar time to luk after yer own.*

Sometimes the Yorkshireman's inclination to obtain something for nothing can lead to confusion. One Yorkshire writer recorded a conversation with a man who thought he'd had a stroke of good fortune:

> *Aw once knew a chap at fan a topcoit, an' he came to me, an' says, "Aa lad! Aw've fun one o' th' grandest topcoits today at iver tha clapt thi' een on."*
>
> *"Why, where did ta find it?" Aw says.*
>
> *"Reight o' th' top o' Skurcoit moor."*
>
> *"Well, tha'rt a lucky chap," Aw says. "What has ta done wi' it?"*
>
> *"Aw niver touched it; Aw left it just whear it wor."*
>
> *"Well, tha art a faoil; tha should ha' brout it hooam."*

*"E'ea! An' Aw should ha' done, but does ta see, ther wor
a chap in it."*

Yorkshire folk also have a reputation for going their own
way; indeed, they are often said to have more pride in
being a native of God's Own County than in their country
or nationality. They have a history of rebellion against
foreign control, reaching back through the Wars of the
Roses, the Norman conquest and successive invasions by
Danish incomers; they have always been a difficult folk to
rule, prompting one Archbishop of York in the 1580s to
complain bitterly of his unruly flock that *A more stiff-necked,
wilful, or obstinate people did I never know or hear of.* It is an oft-
quoted maxim that you can always tell a Yorkshireman
– but you can't tell him much.

The Wars of the Roses, that bloody dynastic struggle
between two branches of the House of Plantagenet, is still
remembered in Yorkshire. The White Rose of York fought
the Red Rose of Lancaster for the throne of England in
a number of vicious battles between 1455 and 1485, with
the Lancastrian Henry Tudor finally emerging the victor.
However, this defeat has never been entirely forgotten or
forgiven, and Lancashire is rarely called by name by a true
Yorkshireman. Instead, it is referred to as *ower t'border,* or
simply *t'other place.*

Like anywhere else in the country there are local rivalries between Yorkshire towns and villages, with many rich examples of dialect illustrating local pride and a bit of mockery at the expense of the folk in the next town – although it should be said that even those derided folk would be preferable to *off-comed-uns*, or foreigners from outside Yorkshire. Halifax is known for its steep hills, and the folk from that town were said to have *Halifax legs* – one leg shorter than the other, the better to walk in a straight line along a hillside. Of course, it is well known that when such folk descend onto flat land they tend to walk in circles. However, the citizens of Halifax retaliated against the people of Heptonstall, near Hebden Bridge, with the following rhyme:

Halifax is built o' wax,
Heptonstall o' stooan.
I' Halifax ther's bonny lasses,
I' Heptonstall there's nooan.

There are two rivers in the West Yorkshire town of Castleford, the Aire and the Calder, and the girls of this town were said to be especially clean and desirable, having two rivers in which to wash and rinse *(sind)* themselves:

Castleford lasses may weel be fair,
For the' wesh i' t'Calder an' sind i' t'Aire.

(I come from a long line of Castleford lasses, so who am I to argue?) However, other towns also boast of their attractive young women; the lasses of Bedale in North Yorkshire were known for their millinery elegance as well as their beauty:

Bedale bonnets an' Bedale faces,
Finnd nowt ti beat 'em in onny places.

The night of November 5th, known in the rest of the country as Guy Fawkes' Night or Bonfire Night, is know in Yorkshire as Plot or Mischief Night. The failure of the gunpowder plot to blow up Parliament and kill James I is celebrated with particular enthusiasm in Yorkshire since Guy Fawkes was a Yorkshireman – he was born and went to school in York, and lived in Scotton near Knaresborough where he converted to Catholicism. However, the custom of burning a guy on a bonfire is not followed in certain parts of the county, notably at St Peter's School in York where Fawkes was a pupil. Plot Night is celebrated with fireworks and parkin, the traditional Yorkshire gingerbread made with oats and treacle, and with plot toffee (sometimes also known as bonfire toffee or treacle toffee).

Children and families

My family hails from Yorkshire – proud Castleford folk all –
and family Christmases and visits 'home' (as my mother still
refers to Yorkshire, despite decades living in East Anglia)
were punctuated with my grandparents' pithy sayings and
dialect pronouncements. I remember my grandmother
berating my father for playing active physical games with
the children at bedtime, winding us up to a pitch of high
excitement: *Give ower, our Roger! Stop towin' abaht, ye'll mek
'em high as kites!* She would also condemn foolish folk for
being *daft as a brush*, and would sometimes shake her head
at the eccentricity of others, murmuring that *there's nowt
so queer as folk.* Yorkshire men may be renowned for their
stubborn and parsimonious ways, but it is well known that
down-to-earth Yorkshire women rule their men with a rod
of iron. A maxim often shared with young wives is that
one should *never put thee 'usband on a pedestal, for e'll nobbut
want dustin'.* Similarly, Yorkshire mothers, while fiercely
proud of their offspring, don't stand for airs and graces.
Joseph Wright was a great pioneer of dialect studies who
began his life as a quarry labourer in Shipley in the mid-
nineteenth century. He taught himself to read and write,
studied at various colleges and universities and ended up
as Professor of Comparative Philology at Oxford, where he
published his English Dialect Dictionary in 1905 – still a

standard reference work. However, his Yorkshire mother was not so easily impressed. He invited her down to Oxford and proudly showed her round the colleges, expecting her to be awed by the architecture and the weight of history. However, when he asked her what she thought of one magnificent edifice she looked up at it and said simply, *Ee, but it'd mek a grand Co-Op.*

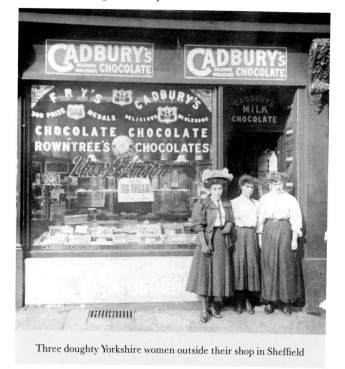

Three doughty Yorkshire women outside their shop in Sheffield

The men sometimes tried to put their women in their place; it was an old country saying that a *whistlin' woman an' a crowin' 'en brings t'Owd Lad aht o' 'is den.* However, it is doubtful whether even the Devil would take on a Yorkshirewoman, whistling or not.

Women had their own clubs and societies, some of which are recorded in the anecdotal writings of authors like Emily Denby, a local journalist who wrote in dialect under the pen name of Buxom Betty in the Bradford Telegraph and Argus. Little of her work remains available, but here is a tale about *t'Owd Maids' Club* returning after an outing, to discover the havoc wreaked by a stray dog they had previously taken in:

> *When they gat back t'dog greeted 'em wi ivvery sign o' joy an' gladness, and they all med a lot on it woll they saw what it had been dewin'. It must ha' felt a bit dowly woll they were aht, cos it hed rooited rahnd and hed comed across a fancy table runner 'at Lizzie hed been embroiderin' wi' gurt blue roses, an' it hed worried it an' chowed it an' shakked it woll you couldn't tell what t' article wor meant for nobbut regs.*

History doesn't record what became of the dog – or the table runner, for that matter.

Yorkshire cuisine is hearty and filling, the product of an agricultural and industrial heritage that required energy and sustenance for the hard physical labour demanded of the local workforce. The county's reputation for parsimony extends to snap as well as brass, however, with no food wasted – as shown in the Yorkshire grace, allegedly recited at tables across the county: *God bless us all and mek us able to eyt all t'stuff that's on this table.*

The county's most famous dish, the Yorkshire pudding, is traditionally served as a starter in its homeland. Rather than the small and rather weedy bun-sized puddings served on the same plate as the main course across the rest of the country, true Yorkshire puddings are plate-sized, full of thick gravy and served as an hors d'oeuvre. The reason for this is that meat was often scarce in working-class households, and Yorkshire puddings were an excellent way of filling up a hungry family before the main course, so that meagre meat rations might stretch a little further. Children were encouraged to eat all their pudding with the promise that *ee as finishes fust gets t'most meat* – rather a crafty move by their canny mothers. My grandmother also insisted that Yorkshire puddings were invented by a cunning Yorkshireman to keep his wife under his thumb. After stoking up the coal-fired oven hot enough to melt steel, and then beating the batter to within an inch of its life (to make the puddings rise and prevent them going sad), the wife had precious little energy left to get uppity and argue back!

Yorkshire fishcakes, sometimes known as patties, were another great delicacy which we used to look forward to with great anticipation during our visits to the West Riding. A Yorkshire fishcake is vastly superior to similar items from different parts of the country, being a slab of fish sandwiched between two slices of potato, the whole thing being then battered and deep fried. There's not much to beat one of these, served with chips, plenty of salt and vinegar and a bag of scraps (the bits of batter left in the fryer), and eaten in the open air out of yesterday's newspaper.

I remember eating chips (and probably a fishcake) standing on the bank of the River Aire just to the north of Castleford and looking at Thomas the Barge – the subject of a well-loved family story and also a local landmark. Thomas was a Tom Pudding-style short coal barge, originally owned by the Holden family, who had plied the local waterways since he was built in Knottingley in 1934. One stormy night in 1977 Thomas was moored upstream of the weir on the Aire when he was untied by vandals unknown. He drifted downstream and over the weir, where he became lodged and has remained ever since. For us, no trip to Yorkshire was complete without a glimpse of Thomas, often caught by craning our necks as we passed over the Lock Lane road bridge on our way to Allerton Bywater and our grandmother's house. Thomas is so much a part of our family history that my nephew is named after him.

Another family story was the tale of Mary Panel (or Pannal), who died in 1603, allegedly the last witch to be burned at the stake in Britain. Mary lived in Ledston, a village to the north of Castleford, and was employed as a maid at Ledston Hall. When William Witham, the son of her employer, fell ill Mary prepared a herbal liniment to treat the boy, but his mother mistakenly gave it to him to drink and the boy was poisoned and died. Mary was accused of bewitching the boy, and was tried and burned (or, in some versions of the tale, hanged) on the wooded hill which now bears her name. Her spirit is believed to haunt the area, and I remember walking along the straight Roman road which leads north out of Castleford and up t'Panel (as my grandmother called the hill), allowing my imagination to recreate the last moments of poor doomed Mary's life as I approached the dark and dense woodland which crowns the hill. Needless to say, I did not linger.

Yorkshire children had a rich vocabulary of rhymes, games and terms. Marbles or taws was a hugely popular game, with complicated rules and many different classes of marbles, from alleys and blood-alleys to dobbies and mabs. The game of *ring-taws* involved trying to knock one's opponents' taws out of a ring placed on the ground, with the loser forfeiting the marbles that were lost. A child who had lost all his marbles was said to be *scoggered*.

Children playing in Darnall, Sheffield

Kick-out can was another children's game, where an empty can was placed in a chalk circle drawn on the ground. One child is nominated to be it, and the others run off and hide. The object of the game is to reach the chalk circle and kick the can outside its boundary without being caught. Adults also had their own sports and games; in *knur and spell* the object was to hit a ball (the knur) as far as possible using a knobbed stick (the pummel). The knur was propelled from a hurling machine (the spell) which was triggered by a sprung lever. This game was popular throughout the nineteenth century, with local leagues and regular reports in newspapers and bulletins across Yorkshire.

The ladybird, always a popular insect with children, was known variously in Yorkshire as a *judycow* or a *ladycow*, and the following rather tragic rhyme was sung to them:

> *Ladycow, ladycow, hie thy way wum,*
> *Thy haase is afire, thy childer all gone.*
> *All but poor Nancy, set under a pan,*
> *Weyvin' gold lace as fast as shoo can.*

Snails were also honoured in the following rhyming couplet:

> *Sneel, sneel, put oot your horn,*
> *Thy fayther an' mutha'll gie ye some corn.*

Birds were part of the rural and urban environment, and Yorkshire dialect contains a wide variety of terms for common (and, these days, not so common) species. The thrush was known as a *throstle* or as *Jeremy Joy*, while the chaffinch was known as a *spink* (and the bullfinch was a *bullspink*). The magpie was known as a *nanpie* or a *pynot* and was thought to bring bad luck, which was averted with the following rhyme:

I cross'd t'pynot an' t'pynot cross'd me,
T'devil tak t'pynot an' God save me.

Harvesting at Stannington, 1899

Industry and agriculture

Yorkshire has a proud industrial heritage, from the coal mining heartland to the textile mills and steelworks that clothed and built an empire. The busy factories and heavily populated industrial areas produced a degree of pollution which is only these days being ameliorated. A family anecdote is that my grandmother was able to tell which way the wind was blowing by sticking her head out of the window of the family home in Robin Hood Street, Castleford and sniffing the air. If she could smell the coke ovens, the malt kilns or the chemical factory, she was safe to put washing out. If she could smell the sharp odour of the acid factory, however, it was best to keep the laundry indoors until the wind changed. The coalfields of Yorkshire once employed a quarter of a million men and women – there was no distinction of gender down the mines in the eighteenth century, and it was often so hot far below ground that workers stripped off, the men working entirely naked and the women stripped to the waist.

Coal-getting in Birley East Pit, Woodhouse, around 1900

They would stop working only to eat their *snap*, a packed lunch transported in a tin for safety, and emerge black and unrecognisable at the end of their shifts.

Although the Yorkshire mining industry is now sadly depleted, it has left a legacy in terms of the dialect terms which have survived. One such phrase is the order to *put t'wood i' t'oile*. This is thought to come from a mining practice of obstructing airflow through the mine by blocking vents with flat wooden boards. Children were often employed to do this, and it was common down the mine to hear the instruction to *put t'wood i' t'oile*, meaning to put the wood in the hole, or block the vents. The usage spread to be applied to doors above ground, so the instruction now means *close that door!*

Yorkshire miners and industrial workers have a proud musical tradition, with the region producing many fine brass bands. Time was when every pit, mill, village and working men's society had its own brass band, providing recreation and companionship for the men and entertainment for the rest of the community. There was a thriving tradition of brass band competitions, with local pride bound up firmly in the success or failure of the band against those from neighbouring areas.

Sometimes these competitions spanned counties and even nations; my own great-grandfather was a member of Castleford Subscription Miners' Welfare Brass Band, mostly made up of miners and formed during the national miners' strike of 1912, which won a series of local and national competitions and eventually travelled to Paris in 1913, achieving first equal place in an international brass band contest and going on to tour the German Ruhr valley. The band returned to Yorkshire before the outbreak of war, but never reformed afterwards because many of the men were killed in the hostilities.

Englische Bergarbeiterkapelle aus Castleford in der Grafschaft Yorkshire 1913.

Castleford Subscription Miners' Welfare Brass Band, 1913, at the time of their tour of Germany. My great-grandfather, William Westmoreland, is second from left on the back row

The fishing industry on the east coast was no less busy, with the herring fleet following the shoals from port to port, through Staithes, Robin Hood's Bay, Flamborough, Bridlington, Filey, Scarborough and Whitby. Herring girls arrived with the fleet to process the catch as it was landed. The girls came from different parts of England and stayed in organised lodgings run by martinet landladies who were ever watchful of the girls' morals, but even so, many of them found husbands and settled in the coastal areas.

There were other marine harvests too; *flithers* or *limpets* were a staple part of a fisherman's kit, used as bait for larger catches, and limpet-pickers worked the beaches up and down the coast. There was local rivalry among them; the workers of Staithes near Robin Hood's Bay were taunted with *Steeas yackers, flither-pickers, 'errin'-guts fer garters!* (Staithes acres, limpet-pickers, herring guts to hold up your trousers!)

The outer pier at Scarborough during the herring season

Smuggling was also a lucrative sideline, with contraband goods coming ashore in the dead of night and being moved up through the villages and towns and onwards into the hinterlands. The four-hundred-mile round trip to the Continent across the stormy North Sea made the illicit business trickier and more risky than in other parts of Britain, but nevertheless there was a brisk to-and-fro trade in sheep and wool (from the Yorkshire Dales) and tea, gin and brandy (from Europe) during the seventeenth and eighteenth centuries. Customs officers did their best to curtail the activity, often greasing the palms of informers and causing local strife, but collusion and the availability of many suitable hiding places in the form of caves and cellars meant that the revenue men were usually a step behind the smugglers.

A local anecdote relates how a Flamborough lad, Robin Jewison, was delivering a horse to the Bending Mule inn in 1844 when he encountered a customs man along the way. The officer asked him if he had seen any smuggling activity, to which the boy replied truthfully that he had seen nothing untoward. They went on their respective ways, and when Robin reached the pub the landlord was nowhere to be seen and his wife explained that he was ill in bed.

However, the sound of men moving kegs in the cellar could clearly be heard.

Much later, on his return journey, Robin encountered a loaded cart with muffled wheels, pulled by horses with muffled hooves, and in the dark he heard the voice of the allegedly poorly landlord:

Nah then, oor Robin, we've seen a lot o' thoo leately, an' we're allus pleased to si thi, but thoo tak oor advice – see nowt an' hear nowt, an' some fine day thi owd granfayther may find summat tiv 'is likin' in 'is corn bin.

Robin went quietly on his way, and sure enough the next day the boy's grandfather discovered that a keg of brandy had mysteriously appeared in his granary.

The Yorkshire Dales are fine and productive farming country, with a proud rural tradition of wool, dairy and meat production. In times gone by shepherds used to have their own counting schemes for reckoning the number of their sheep, often involving marks on sticks or tallies to indicate a particular number of animals (commonly ten or twenty). The tally marks were totalled at the end of the count to give the size of the flock.

Different regions of the country have their own distinct rhymes; the Wensleydale version has Celtic origins, and counts up to twenty like this: *Yan, tean, tither, mither, pip, teaser, leaser, catra, horna, dick, yan-dick, tean-dick, tither-dick, mither-dick, bumper, yan-a-bum, tean-a-bum, tither-a-bum, mither-a-bum, jigger.*

Sheep grazing on Langsett Moor

Of course, farming is critically dependent on the weather, and while the Dales countryside is stunning in bright sunshine, it is also renowned for the wet weather that rolls in from the North Sea, gathering over the hills and clouding the Dales and moors in dank and miserable conditions. Yorkshire farmers are often justified in complaining about the weather, as illustrated in the first verse of this Victorian song:

Rainin' ageean, Ah deea declare,
It's twaa days wet fer yah day fair.
Warse tahmes ner theease was niver seen;
Us farmers 'll be beggared clean!

As well as large agricultural concerns, most village households would also have their own small plot of land where they might raise chickens and tend a vegetable plot. However, sometimes these smallholders' gardens were prone to theft, with produce going missing. One Yorkshire writer recorded a complaint made by a local villager:

There were this chap at considered hissen rayther a sharp en; he'd a bit ov a garden an' some cherry trees in it, an' one mornin' when he gate aat o' bed he fan somdy had saved him th' trouble o' getherin' th' fruit; they'd done it fer him woll he wor asleep. He coom an' tell'd th' tale to me.

"Aa," he said, "if Ah could nobbut find aat who done it, Ah'd transport 'em over th' seah, that Ah wod!"

"Why," Aw says, "tha knows burds is varry fond o' cherries, an' it's happen th' burds."

"Burds!" he said, an' he winked at me varry knowingly. "Burds! Happen they wor burds – but they wor two-legged ens, Aw'll bet!" Aw niver thowt him quite so sharp after that.

Agricultural workers taking a break from raking.
Around the turn of the century

Bibliography

Many writers have celebrated and preserved the Yorkshire dialect, and as a consequence there is a wide variety of resources available. There is a broad range of modern material, written by enthusiastic and knowledgeable folk, but where possible I have tried to go as far back as possible to track down antiquarian sources who experienced the ancient dialect as it was spoken tens or even hundreds of years ago, or to attested literary works which record the local vernacular in the dialogue of the characters. Among the most useful resources have been the following:

BRONTË, E., *Wuthering Heights* (Wordsworth Classics, 1992)

HARTLEY, J., *Yorkshire Ditties,* First and Second Series (Nicholson & Sons)

HARTLEY, J., *Yorkshire Puddin'* (Nicholson and Sons, 1876)

HARTLEY, J., *Yorkshire Tales* (Nicholson & Sons)

HODGSON BURNETT, F., *The Secret Garden* (Wordsworth Children's Classics, 1993)

KELLETT, A. (ED.), *The Little Book of Yorkshire Dialect* (Dalesman, 2008)

KELLET, A. (ED.), *The Yorkshire Dictionary of Dialect, Tradition and Folklore* (Smith Settle, 1994)

MARKHAM, L., *Ee Up Lad! A Salute to the Yorkshire Dialect* (Countryside Books, 2002)

Moorman, F.W., *Songs of the Ridings* (Elkin Mathews, 1918)

Wright, J., *English Dialect Dictionary* (OUP, 1898–1905)

There is also a rich diversity of online resources, which have been collected and collated by many dedicated individuals. Among the most interesting are:

The BBC Voices project:
http://bbc.co.uk/voices/

The Yorkshire dialect pages at Rootsweb:
http://freepages.genealogy.rootsweb.ancestry.com/~maureenmitchell/yorkshire/dialect_words.htm

The Yorkshire Dialect Society:
http://www.yorkshiredialectsociety.org.uk/

Yorkshire Dialect:
http://www.yorkshiredialect.com/

PHOTOGRAPHIC CREDITS

Page No.	Caption and Credit
	Sheffield City Council, Libraries Archives and Information
11	Outcrop mining at Manor Lane, Sheffield during a coal strike in 1912 Sheffield Local Studies Library Picture Sheffield: s03726
16	Cottage garden outside a house in Grimesthorpe, around 1900 Sheffield Local Studies Library Picture Sheffield: s14161
19	Fetching water from Wild Well, Norton Hollow Sheffield Local Studies Library Picture Sheffield: s04196
22	Orgreave Colliery during the 1893 Coal Strike Sheffield Local Studies Library Picture Sheffield: s10716 Photographer – J C Nicholson
25	The Old Cross Scythes pub, Woodseats Sheffield Local Studies Library Picture Sheffield: s06882
32	Haymaking at Creswick's Farm, Crosspool Sheffield Local Studies Library Picture Sheffield: s02587 Photographer - P Fletcher
36	An open-air service in the East End of Sheffield, 1920s Sheffield Local Studies Library Picture Sheffield: s02904 Photographer – Mottershaw Photography
40	A woman walking in Rivelin Valley Sheffield Local Studies Library Picture Sheffield: s12145
44	The pit head at Tinsley Park Colliery Sheffield Local Studies Library Picture Sheffield: u02819
54	Lodge Moor, Sheffield Sheffield Local Studies Library Picture Sheffield: s12087 Photographer – Valentine's Series
6/60	Three doughty Yorkshire women outside their shop in Sheffield Sheffield Local Studies Library Picture Sheffield: v02813

Page No.	Caption and Credit
65	Children playing in Darnall, Sheffield Sheffield Local Studies Library Picture Sheffield: v01863 Photographer – Malcolm Shaw
67	Harvesting at Stannington, 1899 Sheffield Local Studies Library Picture Sheffield: s09660
68	Coal-getting in Birley East Pit, Sheffield Woodhouse, around 1900 Sheffield Local Studies Library Picture Sheffield: t01838
75	Sheep grazing on Langsett Moor Sheffield Local Studies Library Picture Sheffield: s12111
77	Agricultural workers taking a break from raking around the turn of the century Sheffield Local Studies Library Picture Sheffield: s09266
	NYCC Unnetie Digital Archive
4/29	York Minster and city walls 'Copyright NYCC Unnetie Digital Archive'
48	Farming in Robin Hood's Bay 'Copyright NYCC Unnetie Digital Archive'
51	Fishing in the River Swale at Low Row, a village in Swaledale 'Copyright NYCC Unnetie Digital Archive'
53	The Cow and Calf Rocks, Ilkley Moor 'Copyright NYCC Unnetie Digital Archive'
72	The outer pier at Scarborough during the herring season 'Copyright NYCC Unnetie Digital Archive'
	The Author
70	Castleford Subscription Miners' Welfare Brass Band, 1913, at the time of their tour of Germany. My great grandfather, William Westmoreland, is second from left on the back row.